The Professor directs the body's defence system. He and Metro, his lieutenant, work to protect your body. Globus and his team of red blood cells need protection as they travel the body delivering oxygen. So Captain Courageous, chief of the white corpuscles and his friends Ace and Corpo cruise around the body attacking their enemies Virulus, the virus and Toxicus, the bacterium.

CONTENTS

HEALTH AND FITNESS

page **Becoming An Adult**

6   What is adolescence?

8   Reproductive organs

10   Important changes

12   Who is the strongest?

13   Our own opinions

14   Learning about sex

HEALTH AND FITNESS

Coping With Problems

16   Our families

17   Special friends

18   School is not just work

19   Your teacher

20   Eat well

21   A good night's sleep

22   Sport is important

24   Don't drink too much alcohol

25   Choosing a career

26   Sailing

26   Windsurfing

       Plus the Growing Up Quiz

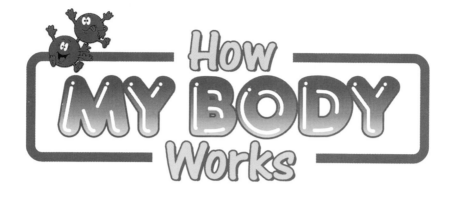

Growing Up

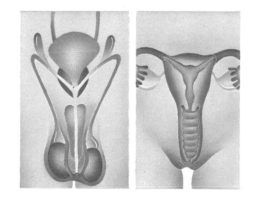

Becoming An Adult

What is adolescence?

Adolescence is when a child changes into an adult. Both boys and girls change physically and mentally as they become older and more grown up. However, everyone is different, so each individual changes at a different rate. The early stage of adolescence is called **puberty**. This is when the body begins to change sexually. Hormones are produced which trigger the development of the sex organs and sexual awareness. Girls usually start puberty before boys. A girl's body begins to change when she is between nine and 13. Most boys begin puberty between ten and 14.

When a person is 18 years old, he or she becomes an adult under the law and is allowed to vote. But being mature, or grown-up, is more than a matter of age. It means being able to behave in a sensible and thoughtful way.

Young people change a lot during adolescence. Boys and girls develop strong opinions about what they like and dislike. They might begin important relationships with the opposite sex, and start a busy social life, going to clubs and parties.

Puberty is the beginning of a new and exciting time. Boys and girls start to have new ideas and develop their own thoughts about the way they would like to live. Puberty can also be an upsetting time if we don't understand what is happening to our bodies. Boys begin to grow hair on their faces and have deep voices and girls develop breasts and have **periods**. All the changes show that we are becoming adults.

During adolescence, boys and girls become more aware of the way they look and may be self-conscious about their bodies. Young people form strong viewpoints and sometimes rebel against their parents and the lifestyles

they accepted when they were children.

These days, childhood is a time for learning new things and going to school. We should also spend time having fun and developing our personalities. However, in the 18th century, life was very different and many children were sent out to work from the age of six onwards. Times were hard, and a large family could not survive unless everyone helped to make money. Children worked as servants or were sent down coal mines or up chimneys. It was not unusual for girls of 14 to be married and having children. Unfortunately, this still happens today in poor countries, where a girl's father can sell his daughter to a wealthy husband.

Do you remember?

Reproductive organs

Every living creature needs to make new life, or **reproduce**, in order that its species will survive. For many plants and animals, reproduction is simply a means of multiplying but for human beings it has an extra meaning. Apart from ensuring that the human race will not die out, sexual intercourse also plays a special part in the relationships between men and women. Partners have sex to show that they love each other.

Male reproductive organs

Most of the male reproductive organs, such as the **testicles** and **penis**, are on the outside of a man's body. The

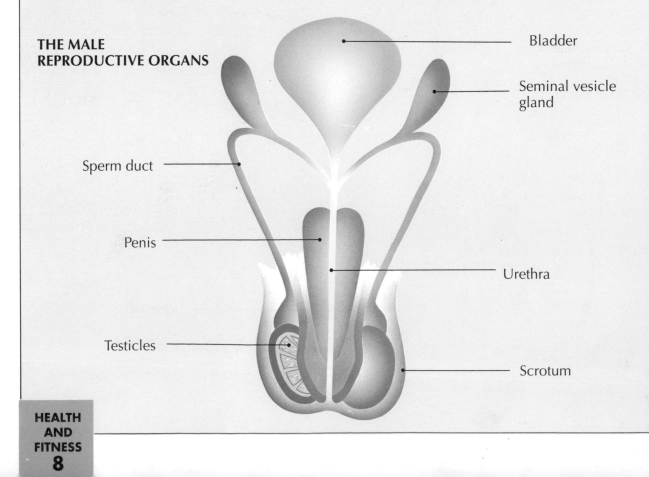

THE MALE REPRODUCTIVE ORGANS

Bladder

Seminal vesicle gland

Sperm duct

Penis

Urethra

Testicles

Scrotum

testicles are two glands where sperm cells are produced. The testicles sit together in a **sac** called the **scrotum**, which hangs between a man's legs. Sperm are tadpole-shaped cells, which can create a new life if they join with an egg in a woman's body.

Three glands – the prostate gland, the seminal vesicle gland and Cowper's gland – together produce a sticky, white fluid which the sperm swim about in. This liquid is called **semen** and it travels through the sperm duct and the urethra, which is a tube running from the bladder to the penis. Semen is squirted out of a man's penis into a woman's body during sexual intercourse.

Female reproductive organs

The female reproductive organs are inside a woman's abdomen. Egg cells are made in the **ovaries**, which are a pair of oval-shaped glands slightly bigger than a man's testicles. However, while the testicles produce millions of sperm at one go, only one egg ripens in an ovary each month. The ovaries are joined to the **uterus** by two tubes – the **Fallopian tubes**. About once a month an egg travels down one of the tubes to the uterus. If it doesn't meet a sperm cell, the body will throw the egg away. This is when a woman has her period. The uterus is linked to the outside of the body by the **vagina**. The opening of the vagina is protected by the **vulva**. A man squirts his sperm into the vagina and they all swim up to the **uterus** to find an egg.

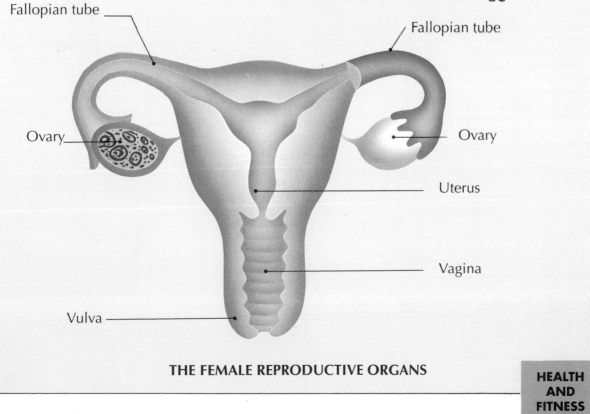

Fallopian tube

Fallopian tube

Ovary

Ovary

Uterus

Vagina

Vulva

THE FEMALE REPRODUCTIVE ORGANS

Important changes

When we grow up, we experience many physical and mental changes. One of the most obvious developments is a sudden increase in height. Children at five years old grow about five to six centimetres a year. When puberty begins, new hormones are produced and the body feels that it is about time it grew a bit faster. Between the ages of ten and 14 both boys and girls shoot upwards – boys tend to grow about nine to ten centimetres and girls usually grow eight to nine centimetres. It is hardly surprising that teenagers find that their clothes don't fit them any more.

During adolescence the body starts producing sex hormones which encourage it to change. Both boys and girls begin to grow hair between their legs, called pubic hair, and under their arms. Some older girls prefer to remove it from their armpits by shaving or using a cream. Girls will begin to develop breasts and start to need a bra. They will

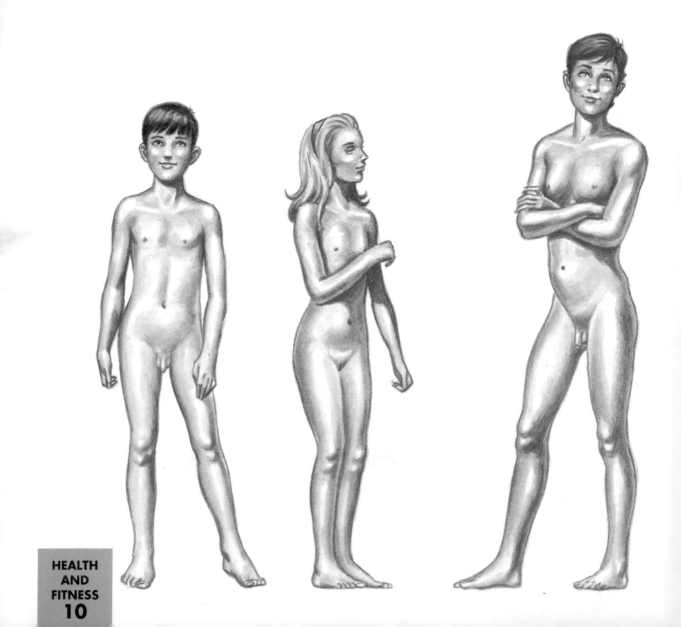

probably have their first **period**, or **menstrual bleeding**, by about the age of 14. This means that they are producing eggs which, if they are fertilised by sperm, can turn into babies.

During puberty our bodies change in many ways. Both boys and girls become taller and begin to grow hair between their legs and under their arms. A boy's penis and testicles become larger, while most girls will develop breasts and their hips become wider.

Boys find that their penis grows bigger and that their testicles hang lower from their bodies. Their voices may become deeper and they might begin to grow facial hair. When they are slightly older they will have to shave every day if they don't want to grow a beard or a moustache. Adolescent boys have their first **ejaculation**, when their penis becomes hard and then releases semen, in their early teens. This means that their bodies are now producing sperm. They have physically reached manhood.

WHO IS THE STRONGEST?

During puberty, all muscles begin to grow and strengthen in boys and girls. For example, heart muscles increase in size to cope with the increase of blood in the growing body. On average, muscles double in size between the ages of ten and 17. Boys' muscles usually grow quicker and twice as big as girl's muscles. However, this does not mean that all boys are stronger than girls. Muscle strength really depends on whether the body is exercised. If a girl keeps herself very fit by swimming, running or aerobics, she could easily be stronger than a boy of the same age.

Each person's muscles grow and strengthen during puberty. However, having big muscles depends on how often we exercise. Lifting weights is a very popular sport for boys, while doing aerobics or gymnastics is more popular among girls.

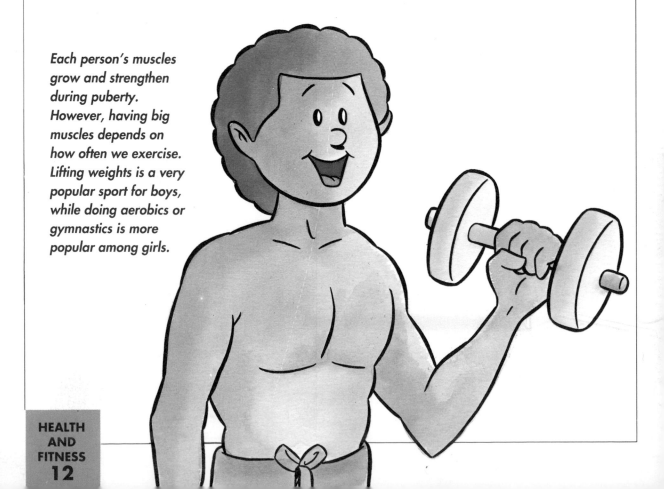

Our own opinions

In the first few years of their lives, children can only understand things they can see or touch. As we grow older, to maybe five or six, we begin to understand simple ideas, as long as they are clearly explained. It is obvious that an adult cannot ask a young child a mathematical question. He would have to make the question fun and explain it, for example, by saying, "If you have one apple and are given two more, how many would you have?"

As we get older and go to school our minds begin to develop. We are able to follow arguments and we become interested in what people think and why they do certain things. Our different experiences help us to solve problems. During adolescence, we begin to form our own ideas and want to make our own decisions. We begin to put forward our own views on important ideas such as right and wrong, how the country is run and how the environment should be cared for. This is all part of growing up.

The little boy on the right is unable to understand complex maths problems. He is not as mentally developed as the boy on the left, who is able to work by computer and has reached a stage where he is beginning to form his own opinions about life.

Learning about sex

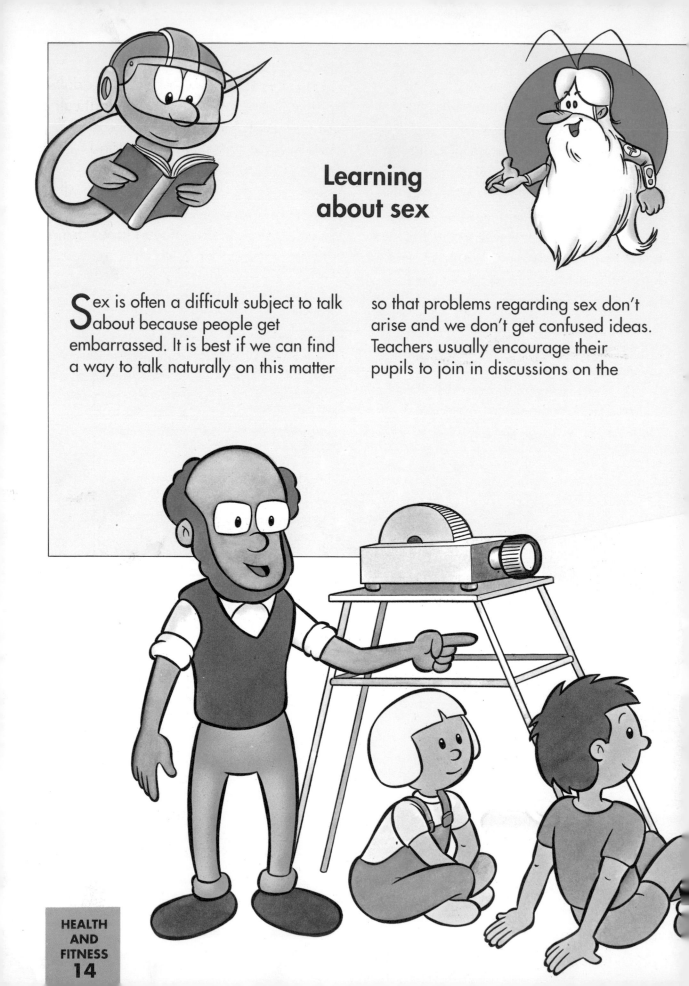

Sex is often a difficult subject to talk about because people get embarrassed. It is best if we can find a way to talk naturally on this matter so that problems regarding sex don't arise and we don't get confused ideas. Teachers usually encourage their pupils to join in discussions on the subject of sex during lessons. It is also helpful if parents are able to talk openly to their children about growing up.

Some schools have lessons for older children which include information about **contraception** – how to avoid having babies – and the importance of loving partnerships. It is also necessary to know about diseases which can be caught during sexual intercourse and how to avoid them.

Everyone, even the most sensible adults you know, has been through the difficult and confusing time called adolescence. We can cope best if we understand clearly how our bodies will change before it happens. Science teachers will tell you about the male and female sex organs, and slides and video tapes are a good way to explain sex.

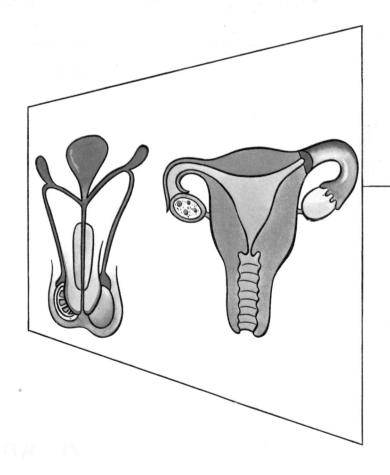

Coping With Problems

Our families

Growing up into a teenager not only brings physical and mental changes. It often leads to changes in attitudes and values. Adolescents begin to see the world with different eyes. Not only do they have opinions that are different to those they had as a child, but they may also disagree with what their parents and other adults think. They are beginning to form their own ideas about life. Arguments between teenagers, parents and other adults are very common.

Adolescents will want to become much more independent, but they still need the protection and support of a caring family. At this time young people may meet another person who they feel very attracted to and may fall in love. Sometimes this is the beginning of a long and happy relationship, but if the other person doesn't feel the same way, it can be very difficult to bear. People have to go through these difficult times to find the right sort of person for them to share their lives with. Some people, in fact, always prefer to live alone.

Growing up is hard to do, and kindly advice is very important for an adolescent. Some adults find it difficult to talk to teenagers, but you should try to find someone who you can talk to, such as a grandparent.

Special friends

Adolescence can be a very enjoyable time. As young people grow up, they go out on their own more often and choose where they go – to the cinema, to parties, to clubs and to sports events. It is the time when close relationships are formed between pairs and groups of people.

Very young children enjoy playing in small groups of children of similar ages. As children get older, their friendship groups often become more organised and they may form gangs with a leader and rules that everyone must obey. They may have special signs and badges. The children are playing at forming their own society and trying out the sort of relationships that, as adults, they will be part of.

Boys and girls both join gangs and groups, but many young people will have a best friend or one or two close chums.

School is not just work

The main reason for going to school is to learn the basics needed for everyday life, such as reading, writing and maths. As young people go on to junior and senior school, they will study different subjects and the school will try to develop each individual's abilities. One person may be good at science, someone else may shine at craft and design, and another person may enjoy foreign languages.

Apart from learning, school is also a place where friendships are made. At school young people learn to be part of a community, where they must care about the needs of others, and learn to accept other people's authority. This is very important for the development of their character.

Even the best school atmosphere can be affected by the pressure of learning and examination results. Many pupils find it difficult to cope with homework or exams. However, the world is full of stressful situations and adolescents need to experience them in preparation for adult life. Knowing what they can cope with will help people to make a suitable choice of career.

Nowadays it is possible for pupils to take part in the organisation and management of school life. They can, for example, help to choose speakers for class and school lectures, and many pupils take part in such activities as planning the school magazine, or arranging special events. These things are all good training for adult life.

Along with providing a good education, schools also encourage pupils to work in groups. This is a good way of learning to appreciate each individual's contribution to a joint activity.

Your teacher

All teachers have a great deal to offer their pupils. They have much knowledge to pass on, and have been to college or university to learn how to teach. In secondary schools in particular, teachers have specialist areas of knowledge, such as science or sport.

Sometimes you may have a teacher that you find difficult. Perhaps you feel he or she is too strict, or you think the lessons are boring. Try to remember that a teacher has an enormous number of pupils to cope with each day, and perhaps he or she finds your class difficult too! Teachers are only human and you need to understand them and join in with the lesson.

When you have a teacher with whom you get on well, in a subject you like, the lessons are enjoyable. It is always in your best interest to make the most of your classes as you will be the one to benefit from what you learn.

Eat well

Taking control of your life also means being responsible for your diet. You need to develop good eating habits so that you are a healthy adult.

● Eat a good breakfast as this gives your body energy for the day ahead.

A cereal which has a high fibre content and lots of vitamins, along with toast and fruit juice is an ideal breakfast.

● An apple or banana is a better snack than a bar of chocolate or crisps.

● A good school dinner or well-planned packed lunch is much better for you than a quick hamburger.

● Sweets should not replace a meal.

● Don't eat your evening meal too late or eat heavy foods that are difficult to digest. This is likely to keep you awake and disturb your sleep. Some people find the caffeine in coffee has a stimulating effect and stops them getting off to sleep. Try not to get into the habit of drinking coffee too often and drink decaffeinated coffee in the evening.

Fast food is high in calories, sugar and fat, but is extremely popular with children and adolescents. Make sure that fast food is only an occasional part of your diet and that the other things you eat are well balanced.

A good night's sleep

People need different amounts of sleep to be at their best. Children tend to need nine or ten hours' sleep each night, whereas adults need about seven or eight hours. Sleep rests your body and restores its energy.

People need to work out how much sleep they need and then organise their lives to be sure they get enough. Those who need a lot of sleep should not be tempted to stay up late too often or they will become run down. If you have friends who need more sleep than you do, be understanding and don't encourage them to stay up late if it doesn't suit them.

Sport is important

Sport, especially when practised as part of a team or a club, encourages social relationships and often leads to close, long-lasting friendships. The strong ties between team members creates a sense of responsibility and encourages trust in others. In this way, the advantages of sport go far beyond physical exercise.

A good sportsperson learns to make sacrifices, to win and lose graciously, to work together with other people and to place the interests of the team before his or her own wishes.

Many sports are enjoyed within clubs where people from different cultural backgrounds may meet. Major sporting events provide a reason for people from different countries and races to get together. If you are lucky enough to be

Nowadays it is possible to practise sport almost everywhere. Most towns and cities have their own sports centre or sports hall. If you have not yet taken advantage of your local facilities, you should go along and see what they have to offer. You are very likely to find a sport you enjoy and to meet new friends.

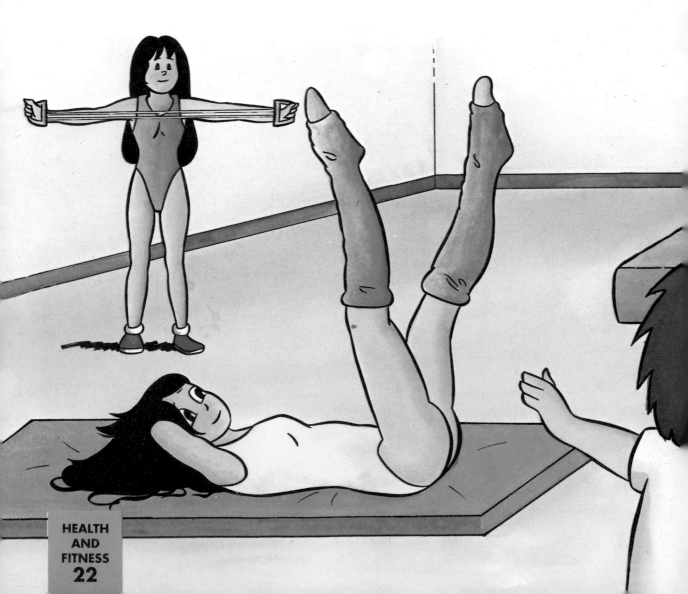

part of an international competition, you may have the opportunity to make friendships with people from far away and learn about their way of life.

Sporting activities are very rewarding in all kinds of ways, not just to develop speed, nimbleness and fitness. Most people can find a sport which they enjoy, and playing sport will be a benefit in their adult life, keeping them fit and active into old age.

Don't drink too much alcohol

In Western countries people tend to drink alcohol at a younger and younger age. Some young people feel they need to drink a lot of alcohol to show how grown-up they are. However, at any age, getting drunk only makes people look stupid and they may actually do stupid, and even dangerous, things.

There is nothing clever about drinking too much alcohol, and if it becomes a habit it can seriously damage the body. In the same way, you should avoid smoking and never be tempted to take drugs. Just because you are growing up, you do not need to try all the bad things associated with adult life.

A person's drink and drug problems are often caused by difficulties at home and at school. However, getting drunk or high on drugs does not solve anything – it only creates further difficulties. A mature person is one who is prepared to face problems and try to solve them.

How stupid these two look because they have drunk too much alcohol. Even if your friends do this, remember it is not a clever, or mature, way to behave.

CHOOSING A CAREER

Some people know from a very early age what job they want to do when they grow up, and never change their mind. This is quite unusual, however, and most young children will think of lots of different jobs they might like.

A child's personality and interests play an important part when choosing a career. If a child gets along well with people, he or she might choose a job in social work or nursing, while a child who enjoys languages might find work as a tour guide. Another child might have a good eye for colour and be very good at drawing and so might choose a more creative job, such as a designer or illustrator.

When thinking about a career, try to consider what you like and dislike and what lessons at school you are good at. This will help you choose the right subjects to study.

KEEPING FIT

• Sailing

Sailing can be practised either as a competitive sport or as a pleasant pastime. Gliding over the water in lovely weather in the company of friends is a great experience. But be careful! What appears simple to an untrained person can easily turn out to be one of the most dangerous sports around. In rough waters and high winds you need to be very strong and fit to handle the sails and steer the boat. You also need expert knowledge so that you do not fall into the water and to prevent the boat from being blown in the wrong direction.

When sailing you need to take care to avoid sunstroke. Sunstroke happens when a person is exposed to strong sun and can cause serious sunburn, a feeling of sickness and a bad headache. Sea-sickness can also make sailing miserable. It is caused by the movement of the boat affecting the fluid in the inner ear, which controls the balance of the body. The symptoms of sea-sickness are dizziness, nausea and vomiting. Many people find they feel sea-sick if they are below deck, but are fine if they keep out in the open air.

Sailing is a sport that the whole family can enjoy. These days, there is a wide choice of sailing boats at different prices which has opened this sport to almost everyone. It is also possible to hire boats and take sailing lessons at lakes. Only sail with experienced people who know the rules of navigation. Everyone who is sailing must listen out for the weather and safety announcements on the radio. You risk your life, and those with you, if you go out to sea in bad weather.

• Windsurfing

A windsurfing board is a light, large surf-board with a sail and a small keel. A windsurfer stands on

Many people love water sports. Sailing and windsurfing demand a high level of skill and strength, and experienced sailors must be mentally alert and have great courage. For many people the sensation of being on the water is very calming and relaxing.

Windsurfing is a popular sport but it can be dangerous if you become careless. Only windsurf if you are a very strong swimmer, and never go too far from the shore.

the board and, by using a wishbone-shaped boom (handle), turns the sail to catch the wind. Standing on the board and controlling the sail requires skill and it is a good idea to have some coaching to begin with. Once the basics are mastered, it is great fun to skim over the waves at the seaside or on a lake.

Windsurfing is a good sport, especially if you also want to sail. It strengthens all the muscles, while also teaching you how to use the wind. However, as with all water sports, you must be extremely careful not to get into danger. You need to be a strong swimmer and keep close to the shore. Never windsurf in bad weather conditions.

KEY WORDS

Adolescence – the stage in human development when a child changes into an adult.

Contraception – the prevention of an egg being fertilised by a sperm cell.

Fallopian tube – the tube which connects the ovary to the uterus.

Ejaculation – the sudden release of semen from an erect penis.

Menstrual bleeding – bleeding from the vagina which occurs about once a month. It is the result of the uterus throwing out its lining and an unwanted egg.

Ovaries – two reproductive organs in a woman's body where eggs are made.

Penis – the male organ used to place sperm in a woman's vagina and also used for urinating.

Periods – the common name for menstrual bleeding, occurring about once a month in girls and women after the body has matured and the ovaries are producing eggs.

Puberty – the stage at the beginning of adolescence when the sex organs begin to develop.

Reproduce – to make new members of the same species; in humans, to make a baby.

Scrotum – a sac of skin containing the testicles.

Semen – a sticky fluid that the sperm swim in.

Testicles – the male reproductive organs where the sperm are made.

Uterus – also called the womb; the reproductive organ in a woman where an unborn baby grows.

HOW MY BODY WORKS

HOW MY BODY WORKS is an educational series that builds into a complete encyclopedia of the human body. Each volume introduces and explains one of its mysteries.

In Part 46 of How My Body Works, you've found out how the body and mind change during adolescence.

Part 47 investigates how we should keep ourselves fit and healthy.

READ ALL ABOUT:
● **Good posture** and how it prevents damage to our spine.
● **The right choice of shoes** so that our feet do not hurt us.
● **Muscle pains and cramps.**
● **Body shapes** – which one are you?

Albert Barillé (pictured left) is the author of this fascinating series of books. The human body is a series of complex systems and mechanisms, so to make it easier for you to understand how the body works, Barillé created The Professor, Captain Courageous, Globus, Toxicus and Virulus, plus many other colourful cartoon characters, to show you around. The Professor and his friends guide you through the body, explaining how it works in a clear and simple way that makes it fun.

TEST YOUR KNOWLEDGE
The Growing Up Quiz

More than one answer may be correct

1. Who starts puberty first?
a) boys
b) girls
c) boys and girls start at the same time

2. At what age does a person become an adult under the law?
a) 16
b) 18
c) 21

3. What happens in puberty?
a) boys begin to grow hair on their faces
b) boys develop deeper voices
c) girls start to have periods

4. What do the testicles sit in?
a) semen
b) a sac called the scrotum
c) the uterus

5. How many glands take part in making semen?
a) 5
b) 3
c) 2

6. How many eggs ripen in an ovary each month?
a) millions
b) 22
c) 1

7. How much do boys and girls grow, on average, between 11 and 14?
a) about 20cm
b) about 9cm
c) about 5cm

8. What is contraception?
a) being very difficult
b) going against your parent's wishes
c) avoiding having babies

9. Which is the best sort of snack?
a) an apple
b) a bar of chocolate
c) a packet of crisps

10. How much sleep does an average adult need?
a) 2 to 3 hours
b) as much as possible
c) 7 to 8 hours

ANSWERS to the **'How My Body Works'** Growing Up Quiz are in Issue 47.
Answers to Issue 45
1 (a), 2 (c), 3 (b), 4 (a & b), 5 (b), 6 (a & b), 7 (b), 8 (a), 9 (b), 10 (c)

Published by
ORBIS PUBLISHING,
Griffin House,
161 Hammersmith Road,
London W6 8SD

BACK ISSUES
Back issues can be obtained by placing an order with your newsagent or, in case of difficulty, from our back numbers department. All cheques/postal orders should be made payable to Orbis Publishing Ltd.

BACK ISSUE CHARGES
Volume 1:
UK: 99p plus £1.00 p&p;
Eire: IR£0.99 plus £1.00 p&p
Thereafter:
UK: £2.99 plus 50p p&p;
Eire: IR£3.50 plus 50p p&p

ADDRESS FOR
BACK ISSUES:
Orbis Publishing Ltd, Unit 10, Wheel Lane Business Park, Wheel Lane, Westfield, Hastings, East Sussex, TN35 4SG. Tel: 0424 755755

BACK ISSUES OVERSEAS
Please place requests for copies of back issues with your newsagent or, in case of difficulty, please write to the relevant address given:

Australia
Gordon and Gotch Ltd, PO Box 290, Burwood VIC 3125 (Enclose cover price plus $1 p&h per issue)

New Zealand
Gordon and Gotch (NZ) Ltd, PO Box 584, Auckland.

South Africa
Back issues Dept
Republican News Agency
PO Box 16034
Doornfontein 2028

Malta & Singapore
Back numbers are available at LM1.50 from your newsagent.

© Procidis Albert Barillé
© 1994 Orbis Publishing Ltd, London
N46 94 06 09
ISBN 0 7489 1043 3
Printed in Italy
by Officine Grafiche De Agostini, Novara